Comforting Little Hearts

Understanding Divorce

Why Don't We Live Together Anymore?

Written by Robin Prince Monroe
Illustrated by Carol Ackelmire

CPH
SAINT LOUIS

Comforting Little Hearts
Series Titles

Why Don't We Live Together Anymore? (Understanding Divorce)

When Will I Feel Better? (Understanding Chronic Illness)

I Have a New Family Now (Understanding Blended Families)

Balloons for Trevor (Understanding Death)

Scripture quotations taken from the HOLY BIBLE, NEW INTERNATIONAL VERSION®. NIV®. Copyright © 1973, 1978, 1984 by International Bible Society. Used by permission of Zondervan Publishing House. All rights reserved.

Copyright © 1998 Robin Prince Monroe

Published by Concordia Publishing House
3558 S. Jefferson Avenue, St. Louis, MO 63118-3968
Manufactured in the United States of America

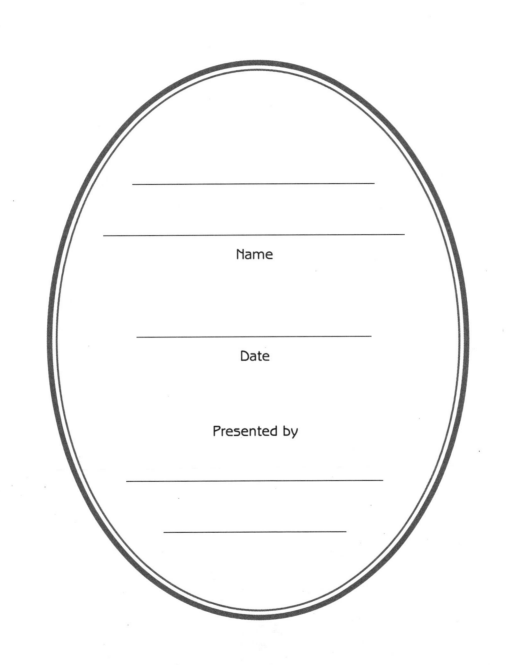

Name

Date

Presented by

In memory of my father
Frank Prince
A.I.A. Architect

Sometimes parents stay married—
even if they argue a little,
even if they get mad at each other,
even if things aren't perfect.

But sometimes parents can't stay together no matter how hard they try. When that happens, they decide it is better to live apart.

One of them moves to another home. This is called being *separated*.

My name is _____.

My parents separated on _____.

Sometimes after parents separate they get a *divorce*. A divorce means that parents are not married anymore.

Write the names of children you know whose parents are divorced.

_____

_____

_____

When families are used to being together, it can be hard being apart. Parents and children will have lots of feelings.

Some children feel *sad*. They miss their together family.

They might cry—they might cry a lot. It is okay to cry. Did you know Jesus cried? He did.

When Jesus saw her weeping ...
He was deeply moved in spirit
and troubled. ... Jesus wept.
John 11:33, 35

Some children get *mad.* It makes them angry that their parents won't stay together.

It's okay to be mad. Did you know Jesus got angry? He did.

Some children feel *bad.* They don't feel like themselves. They feel like something is wrong. They don't feel like crying—they just don't feel very good. Jesus understands those feelings too.

Some children feel *relieved.* Sometimes parents are so unhappy that being separated makes everyone feel a little better.

God loves you no matter how you feel, and you won't feel this way forever.

Tell God how you feel. Listen to the promise He gives you.

So do not fear, for I am with you;
do not be dismayed, for I am your God.
I will strengthen you and help you; I will uphold
you with My righteous right hand.
Isaiah 41:10

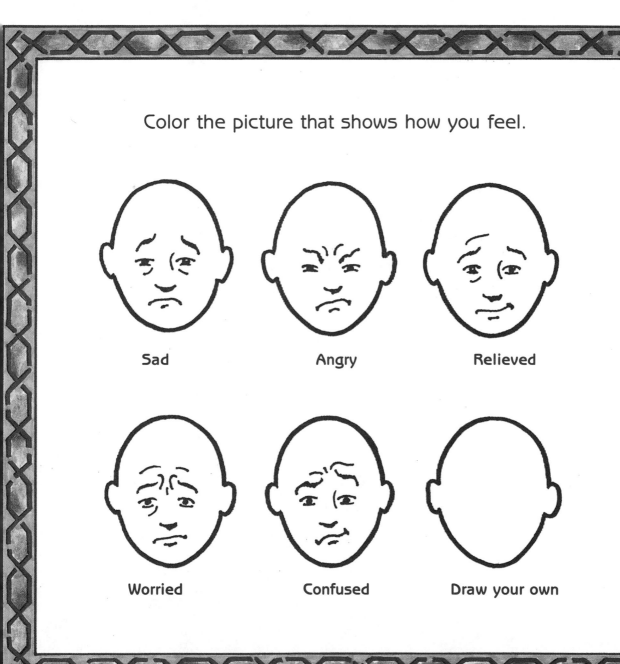

Do you know that God understands exactly how you feel? Do you know He cares about your feelings? He does.

You will feel better if you talk about your feelings with someone who cares about you. Maybe your mom or dad. Maybe your brother, sister, or friend. Maybe a teacher, pastor, or someone at church.

I can talk to_____ about my feelings.

You can talk to God about your feelings too. He is *always* ready to listen.

Divorce happens because we live in a sinful world. But God sent His own Son, Jesus, to take the punishment for that sin and all the other wrong things we do.

Sometimes children think divorce is their fault. But a marriage is only between parents. It is **NEVER** a child's fault when parents decide to divorce.

Say this out loud:

It is not my fault.

Louder:

It is *not* my fault!

Divorce brings a lot of decisions. Your parents will decide where you will live. If parents need help making a decision, a judge may help them. They may ask you how you feel. Be honest with them.

I live with my **mom / dad** most of the time.
(circle one)

This is when I visit my **mom / dad** : _____
(circle one)

_____

Use **purple** to color the days you will be with your mom.

Use yellow to color the days you will be with your dad.

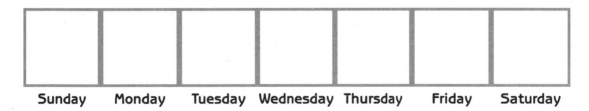

Sunday	Monday	Tuesday	Wednesday	Thursday	Friday	Saturday

You might want to buy a special family calendar and color it each month.

Divorce means a lot of changes. It usually means there will be less money. Having less money may worry you. But you don't need to worry. God promises to take care of you, and He *never* breaks His promises.

Consider how the lilies grow. They do not labor or spin.
Yet I tell you, not even Solomon in all his splendor was dressed
like one of these. If that is how God clothes the grass of the field,
which is here today, and tomorrow is thrown into the fire,
how much more will He clothe you. ...
And do not set your heart on what you will eat or drink;
do not worry about it. ...
Do not be afraid, little flock, for Your Father
has been pleased to give you the kingdom.

Luke 12:27–29, 32

Divorce often means that you will have to move. People have to move for many different reasons. If you think of moving as an adventure, it won't seem nearly as scary.

I **did / did not** have to move.
(circle one)

My new address is: _____

_____

My new phone number is: _____

This is what I miss about my old home: _____

_____

I really like this about my new home: _____

_____

_____

Another change that divorce may bring is that your mom or dad may start *dating*. Dating is when a man and woman spend time together to get to know each other better. This might make you feel uncomfortable.

Maybe you are worried that your mom or dad will not love you as much if they start liking someone else—but love doesn't work that way. We can love more and more people and always have enough for everybody. The more people we love, the bigger our love gets. That's because God fills us with His love.

My mom **is / is not** dating someone. (circle one)

My dad **is / is not** dating someone. (circle one)

My mom's new friend's name is _____.

My dad's new friend's name is _____.

I like this about my mom's new friend _____

_____.

I like this about my dad's new friend _____

_____.

We know and rely on the love
God has for us. God is love.
Whoever lives in love lives
in God, and God in him.
1 John 4:16

When families separate it hurts. You have pain if you break your arm. It is an outside pain. When a family is broken, there is pain too, but it is an inside pain. Just like a broken arm heals, the hurt inside you will heal.

God sees your inside hurt. He loves you, and He will stay close to you. He will help you feel better again. One day you will be able to say, "Divorce *is* hard, but I am just fine now!"

*O Lord my God, I called to You
for help and You healed me.
Psalm 30:2*

How Parents Can Help

by Bitsy Counts,
LISW, LMFT, Family Counselor

Tell your child the facts about your divorce. It is more unsettling to wonder what happened than to know the truth. When explaining the facts, avoid blaming your ex-spouse. Make sure your child knows that he is not the cause of the divorce.

Respect your child's feelings. Everyone going through the divorce, including your child, is grieving. Allow your child to express her feelings appropriately.

Give your child space when he is going from one parent's house to the other's. It is normal for your child to go through a period of adjustment when he leaves for visitation or returns home. This period may last a few hours or a couple days.

Provide structure but be flexible. Daily routine and regular visitation times provide security for your child, but it is also important to make exceptions for special events.

Cooperate with your former spouse regarding child-care issues. The more cooperation your child experiences between her parents regarding visitation, school functions, holidays, etc., the easier her adjustment will be.

Encourage your child to have a positive relationship with your ex-spouse. Your ex-spouse is still your child's parent—he needs *both* of you.

Be your child's parent, not her friend. Resist the temptation to make your child your confidant. She needs you to be a responsible parent.

Avoid making your child a messenger. Don't ask your child to take information to, or bring information from, your ex-spouse. If information needs to be exchanged, do it yourself.

Reminisce with your child. Remember together happy family times during your former marriage. The positive memories will help heal the hurt of the family separation.

Offer your child hope. Encourage your child that his pain will pass, that he will feel better, that he will adjust. Point out any positive results of the change.